INSTRUCTIONS FOR THE DESERT

For Will and George

Also by Cynthia Fuller

Moving Towards Light (1992)

INSTRUCTIONS FOR THE DESERT

Cynthia Fuller

FLAMBARD

ACKNOWLEDGEMENTS

Some of these poems have appeared in the following publications:
All Lombard St to a China Orange, Iron, Other Poetry,
Poetry Durham, St Oswald's Hospice Anthology.

The cover photograph, taken in New Mexico, is by Rob Sargent.
The photograph of Cynthia Fuller is by Tess Spencer.

Cynthia Fuller gratefully acknowledges the award of a Northern Arts Bursary
in 1993, which helped her to write this collection of poems.

Flambard Press wishes to thank Northern Arts for its financial support.

Published in 1996 by Flambard Press
4 Mitchell Avenue, Jesmond, Newcastle upon Tyne NE2 3LA

Typeset by Pandon Press Ltd, Newcastle upon Tyne
in association with Mary Holcroft Veitch
Printed in Great Britain by Cromwell Press, Broughton Gifford,
Melksham, Wiltshire

A CIP catalogue record for this book is available from the British Library
ISBN 1 873226 16 0
© Cynthia Fuller 1996

CONTENTS

INSTRUCTIONS FOR THE DESERT

Going into the desert there will be
no distraction. The sun at its height
will bleach and burn until you cannot see,

and there is no cold like a desert night.
You will know only darkness and rock
unyielding. You will long then for light.

Early morning with the risen sun at your back
will be the best time, the landscape's grey
dyed crimson, rock split to reddening cracks.

You will see the bones, bright white, stray
scatterings as if the flesh had changed its mind,
unhooked, discovering a different way.

Do not think about the bones at night, find
pictures of rare desert blooms, soft contours,
rock folded upon rock, bones will remind

you of fear, fierce birds circling. Remember
it is peace you come looking for, bare truth
in a place without compromise. Never

try to make the rocks speak. The sky's smooth
blue says nothing. When you know how alone
you are, a voice will begin to sing through
blood, through spirit, and through bright white bone.

THE DESERT SPEAKS

They come with their heads
full of miracles. Revelations.
Forty days to sort it out.
Each comes alone. Each follows
a path that is not there, hears
voices in the silence, starves,
hallucinates what is most
desired, most feared, burning.

I have seen skin split, lips swell.
There is death in the sun, death
in the night. The wind blows away
their tracks. Flesh dries. Beak and claw
strip the bones. Skeleton burning.
Tibia, pelvis, knuckle, rib
scattered. Baked white they
dessicate, break down, fine grain.

Beyond even the power of
Ezekiel's god, white flecks
in sand escape resurrection.
The miracle in the earthquake
is what they come looking for,
the shudder of rebirth, bones
reconnecting, another go at
the mystery, a different version.

Do they think they choose?
Ezekiel had a part in someone
else's story. Would Elijah
have seized on earthquake,
wind and fire, given the choice?
Prophet has a ring about it, like
visionary, sibyl. What about pariah?
Outcast. Exile. Derelict.

Welcome to the wilderness,
hermit, outlaw, scapegoat, seer.
No flesh is tolerated.
The soul has many skins.
In the fire of its flaying
will be punishment or relief,
purgation, purification,
the eternal desert of fear.

WHAT THE FOSSIL TELLS

You came looking for god in the landscape,
wind-sculpted rock, time's mystery stratified
in layers of colour, sand, shale and clay.
You wanted your breath taken away,
to be stunned, heart stopped by stern beauty.
You forgot about survival.

Small creatures curl beneath hot rock,
lives slowed down to a faint flutter.
Plants lose all moisture, suspended.
You can believe in gods here, this is
the hundred year sleep, the turning to stone.
The flames of hell are licking your soles.

Your mouth cannot salivate.
There is a hook in your throat that catches.
Your eyes scratch in raw sockets.
Hot dust crusts your nostrils. The cracks
in your swollen lips have healed, split open.
Your skin is thin paper you cannot shed.

Such fire will bake you to orange clay.
You see networks of rills,
underground tunnels opening moist,
the veins of streams branching
from a central current whose roar
you almost hear as you scan bare sky.

You cannot adapt to this place.
Sucked of all moisture you crack.
You will be husk, vacant shell.
There is torture in gullies and sediment,
the sandy bottoms of ephemeral streams,
constant reminders of absence.

There is only the longing, the waiting
for rain. Sudden storm. Flood. Renewal.
Then waiting for rain. Drought's ache
the last trace of desert's lost memory,
and a sea urchin flowering in hot rock,
fossilised star points unlocking.

SHE VISITS THE ORACLE

1

Forty days of hot air
before I found you
unsteady vision.
That smell is the scorch of skin.
See my soles, red garish
as a skinned rabbit.
It was further than I thought.
Sandals melted
footprints burnt away.
I will leave no track.

I mistook the spadefoot toad
for you, the scorpion,
the sidewinder.
Shapechanger, I could be
speaking to the wind.
This is my mind, a seedball
borne by the air.
Each word is spined.
See, my hooked thoughts
detach, depleting.

I found my heart, dried out,
a grey moss. You think
it dead? I tell you,
rain would return
the woody crust to plush.
But not in this season.
I wound my body in black cloth.
The flesh dessicated,
shrunk to the bone,
skin turned reptilian.

I dreamed you as lion body,
head of a golden bird,
sun striking fire
from you metal plumage,
stern forelegs, claws curled.
I saw my body flagging,
last energy snuffed out,
the hook of your beak.
I offered you three
miracles in payment.

2

I did not expect a pillar of sand,
a dust devil whirling.
Are you close, or on the horizon,
oracle or mirage?
Like all the rest, I have
a question but I will
not cut a warm throat for you.
According to the custom
I bring three gifts. Mine are
from desert air, rock, dust.

Wind lifts the surface sand
ripples skims shifts
the layers, uncovers at my feet
in a cluster, roses,
sand roses, pink-gold petals
crystallised to a brittle curl;
sun-baked flowerheads,
a scent of dust,
wind-sculpted blooms.
This is my first token.

At the distant rock face
a skyline of rectangles,
dark squares of window,
a modern city in the desert
where every sand grain
is the past. Hurry
towards its shelter.
It fades, outline melts
back to rock: my second token,
the charm of illusion.

In the night's coldest hour
a flutter of wings,
small movements in darkness,
a delicate stretching.
The cacti are flowering,
releasing wild petals,
wax stars with deep centres.
By dawn they are dead,
a shrivel of ragged colour.
This metaphor my third token.

No sign. Silence. The words
drift. Are you even listening.
No levity. I want an answer
to the hardest question.
It was worth mind, heart, body.
I have been sandblasted, scoured.
Days have burnt away
the skin of habit, nights
shown me a cold vastness
the other side of fear.

I want to know what I would
see if I could see further.
The human mind spawns thoughts
from within its confines
trying to reach beyond them.
But thoughts can only pace
the mind's borders.
Beyond is beyond them.
Take me over the border.
Allow me to see.

3

If I dare to open my eyes
will it be the same?
I have slept curled tight,
sand settled around me.
My fingers are clutching
the stiff black of my garment.
Something is receding,
a door closing on image,
sensation. Can I hold it
back a little longer?

I came for a glimpse
of omniscience, wanting
new understanding,
a shot of godlike vision.
Something did happen.
There was another life –
a scuttling small life –
terrible urgency –
a will to survive –
and then the rain.

Did I stir as slow drops
sizzled on hot rock,
scramble from the crevice,
skin splitting, pushing free?
I remember a stream bed
filling, overflowing, sand
to mud, the relief of moisture;
a tide of desire, to mate,
to lay eggs in the water
before the stream hissed, misted.

Was there a storm
with this rock baked dry,
this sky its fiercest blue?
I think I was a creature
brought to life by rain.
Life and procreation
in the sudden rain.
Touché. What did I expect?
An answer in the thunder?
Illusion or metaphor, you win.

THAT BLUE

'... that Blue that will always be there ... after all
man's destruction is finished.' (Georgia O'Keeffe)

All she takes is an image of her own dust,
teeth that will not burn, knobs of bone.
The city does not see her passing.
Crying is drowned out, sores hidden
in the crowd. There is no time to wonder
who is missing when no one is safe.

Her compass is broken, the needle
dances a wild circle and north is lost.
Maps are history. Painstaking
cartographers believed they traced truth.
Bombs mortars mines kalashnikovs
alter the figurations, landmarks.

Trust only your own eyes, your pulse,
the track underfoot. Forget certainty.

She knows she is some kind of pilgrim.
Already footsore, she dreams thonged sandals,
dust grey between the toes, hot baked rock.
There is no one with her on the path,
no silent figures, no stout staffs, no prayers.
No shared purpose. There is no one to tell.

She is making for the place beyond
which she cannot go. She will know it.
In dreams it is deep in the earth's hot core.
She must head south towards the centre,
moving through the landscape that is known,
that tells her she is leaving, fleeing.

Keep the setting sun on your right.
The patterns of the stars you can trust.

They have been harvesting. Stilled machines
bulk in the darkness. The night air
is sweet with cut stalks. She is
a grey shadow slipping through.
For the last time these fields stretching,
the old trees with familiar roots.

Tugged from this late summer she aches
with leaving. Loss screams in a gull's cry,
land falls away to sea, dark tides lifting.
She is carried through the long night as if
there will be no morning, as if this
is the place beyond which she cannot go.

Look for the grey lightening in the west.
This is not the end of the journey.

Dawn sets her on a dry plain. Dust.
With the sun comes colour, the earth
tints of aridity. Hot red hills
cracked open, the sun a fireball
scorching vegetation, turning soil
to ashes where no roots can hold.

Absence of water quivers in the air.
Tongue and lips are stiffening, moisture
drawn out. She cannot touch the rocks.
Nothing to cast a shadow. No rest.
A high pitched humming vibrates her skull.
There is no way across this plain.

Avoid the sun at its highest point.
Look for the earth's deepest cracks.

She sees her bones then, bleached cool
white before the heat powders them –
the image slipping as she stumbles
into space, comes back to no breath,
trips, falls where only her heart beat
moves. There are high walls, a crack of sky.

The rock soothes, its grey soft as doves.
Rest. The sun does not reach the fissure's depths.
Slow steps. The path shifts underfoot.
Her fingers loose a flurry of small stones.
Just space between the walls to give her passage.
Why not stop here in this narrow place –

Trust only your own eyes, your pulse,
the track underfoot. Forget certainty.

The path twists upwards pulling her on.
She cannot look ahead or she will fall.
She feels a flicker, a touch, not on skin –
at her centre – her heart, is it, her mind?
There is an opening ahead as if
a doorway had been cut into the rock.

She stands at the lintel, straightens.
She sees only blue. A clear summer sky
blue azure aquamarine cobalt
stretching no horizon no line no edge
to break the infinite. She can leave
her dust at the threshold, step through.

CAVE

1

From wars burning, despair
crying that there is no love,
she slips through the earth's crack

from light into darkness.
Crouched naked on the rock shelf,
the chamber hugs her close.

She is cool pale – reptile? –
an ancient sea creature
beached breathless in this cave.

She curls tight. Her limbs
will be simple coils petrified
in the rock's moist cold.

She surrenders her body
to the stone but her soul
will not give up

searching for compassion
in soldiers' eyes, for love
in the hearts of the dead.

2

She is learning to breathe
shallowly, lungs no longer filling,
the bones of her chest almost still.

She feels the blood tracking
slowly, colder and she
pictures it as blue, cold blue.

She is practising not moving,
dreams she hovers outside
her body's curled stone.

For the world is a stern place.
Hope flickers out. We let
the children die.

Has love, community,
put only weapons in our hands?
She cannot keep faith

with life. She is almost stone.
She hears the soft wings brushing,
brushing in the cold.

NIGHT THOUGHTS

Tonight the sky is clear again, space
cold and dark between the stars, earth
dwarfed by night, small struggles lost
as distance opens, stretches, and time
is not tomorrow, nor a life, but infinite,
the currents of an ocean pulling.

So many deaths, fresh hatred pulling
at the heart, bewildering; no space
for mourning, loss is infinite,
has hasty burial, the earth
smoothed over. There is no time
to grieve, to know what has been lost.

Each cruel act, each hurt is lost
in the next atrocity, tomorrow pulling
from today, dragging us along time's
tunnel, small scratching creatures, and space
a vastness where the cries of earth
are silent, no ripple in the infinite.

We cannot look for help in the infinite
night, as if out there we'd find a lost
thread that held it firm, that made the earth
someone's idea of paradise. As if the pulling
of a thread undid us, made a space
for greed and hate and filled our time

with tyranny and war. We shaped this time
that starves the spirit, makes infinite
the suffering, gives good no space
to breathe. Now innocence is lost
and love's bright thread is cut, pulling
us one from another, making of earth

a wasteland where roots in parched earth
wither. Our lives make not a wrinkle on time's
skin, yet are all we have, fear pulling
at the edges of our dreams. The infinite
sky does not need us, we are lost
children who face only darkness, space.

Small spinning earth, the infinite
makes our sad time a beat that's lost
between the current pulling and cold space.

WINTER LIGHT

What has it done, the winter light
with its opalescence and cold edge?
Day lengthening it drained all colour
to still silver, black lines, grey darkening.
What has it leeched from us who sat
soaking in its pale beauty?
We are bleached like bare bone; cold, so cold.

DALES DECEMBER

The land folds soft, streams cut
deep channels in thick turf.
Only the sheep keep a wild eye
on me; they are rough grey stone.
Stone barns, stone walls, mark out
old boundaries, old paths,
the air so cold and pure it hurts,
strips back to blood and bone:
the flowering clarity of pain.
Not much has changed here.
Winters have always driven
us inward towards the centre.
I will be scoured by sleet,
gripped by ice, until I see.

LANDSCAPES

In this flat land the sun is heavy,
pulling to earth at afternoon's midpoint,
letting back the chill. Night frost persisted,
ice splinters the soft crumble of furrow.
The landscape is certain, angled exact,
even paths edge the field's square,
trees ink black lines across cold sky.

Where conversation takes us has no map,
no measured contours, no marked path.
If others came this way before, they left
no trail, no smoking ash, no messages.
Past my midpoint, an anxious pioneer,
I need a compass, my unwieldy pack drags,
smooth rock resists my stumbling tracks.

Talk can unsettle worlds,
make of the mind a solitary place.
Caught in our separate landscapes
our steps quicken, dusk washes
solidity to shadow, edges blur.
An urgent journey, the final route,
before darkness drowns the ebbing light.

MUNGRISDALE COMMON

A bitter wind has parched the land,
paled greens, scattered bleached tussocks,
dry husks, across the greying slope.
Earth shuddered and the safe ground gaped.
The ridge's flesh is grazed, scraped back
to rock. The skyline tells of violence.
On paths of shattered slate a spring
breaks through, blackening the blue-grey
to a wet roof sheen. A hush in the bent grass.
A raven's hollow cough says death, the sky's
blue lures to the fissure's edge,
under the mad striped gaze of sheep.
Go back to the lime green splashes on the rock.
Ghosts may be displaced by a lark's song.

Once we were lost here. The path sank
beneath spongy ground. Drowned. Summer
stretched the day out and we found a way.
These could be our ghosts that are touching me,
pulling to the top of the ridge.
They want to show us our small selves below,
circling the common, always lost. Time's trap
caught us before the path appeared, forever
circling, the cotton grass marking nothing.
Too quiet. All sorrow held until
I think the sky is aching, for all its blue.
Death is in the wind, and where are we?
Haunted by our ghosts, who are we now
who thought we could walk these ways again?

PATHS

There are always walls,
stones well settled,
cut grey weathered to grey-green
lit by the mustard of lichen,
walls dividing crops from meadow,
portioning the land.
The paths are different.
Uneven ways recall
other feet that stumbled
seeking out smooth surfaces.
The bulky packhorse
threading between farms,
heavy-uddered cows,
sheep with panic eyes
caught between walls
for centuries. Long skirts,
stout boots, at dusk
you feel them pass here,
soft as moths.

Smoother paths let you see
the late summer of cut corn,
old trees shadowing a pool,
a landscape benign, familiar,
quiet farms and gentle streams.
But above you rocks edge to crags,
cut dark against the sky.
Clouds drift covering,
uncovering bare ridge,
in the lee of the hill
the safe path shrinking.
Is this what they buried
under concrete in grey cities,
buildings tilting at the sky,

creating other fears
to cover this, another silence
stirring on night streets
to drown out the vastness
of earth and sky.

There is always this following
of paths, making our way
between walls, looking down,
back, inward, ahead, upward,
searching for destinations,
resting places, silence.
One path will end
at the deserted garden,
where sheltering walls are broken,
the arch where the door opened
remains, the paths between beds
lost, tame plants grown wild.
Much could be salvaged here, restored.
The higher path will bring you out
on the grey crag in cold cloud.
You will breathe fear, know
your temporary heart,
your body no more than the raven,
the bracken, marsh grass, stone.

BARN

Your going leaves a space that gapes,
a barn where timber settles in the roof.
Small lives scuffle in the shadows, the birds
that skimmed and squealed away the summer grew
wings strong enough to cross continents,
and left. In its steady arch the door is closed.
A solid wooden beam is latched across.
I stand afraid to open to such darkness.

That barn floor should be swept and sweet
to house the neat packed bales of summer.
Fat bellied sacks of grain should nudge in rows.
The apples should be set in line, close
but not touching; the reluctant pears
would soften here. And on the shelves
should glisten jars of fruit, their sweetness
caught, preserved, against such a time.

I knew the rules and did not listen.
Here is nothing stored against the darkness,
harvest is absence. This barn is bare.
In dreams I catch a wingbeat, heavy, distant,
a certain cry: no soft-feathered murmur,
domestic squawk, no barn fowl that wild call.
Slide back the beam, open the wooden door,
whatever fierce visitor will winter here.

METAPHORS

Perhaps it was simply that we walked
too far, nothing more, so that the sun
sank below the ridge as curlews
circled us with their sad cry; birds sang
from the safety of night perches; the lambs
we woke skittered white wool in dim fields
like ghosts, and, tired, we had to quicken
heavy legs against the warm day's
legacy of chilling mist, and darkness.

Perhaps I chose then to remember
the sheep hurrying her lambs away
through the rough tussocks, leaving in
our path the afterbirth glistening,
the shock of the membranes, flame-red silk.

APRIL

Winter is convincing about death,
dark tides and sleet in the wind
close the heart to faith.
We cannot believe in spring
with the earth locked hard.
Only with the budding,
the first shoots gleaming
does memory stir, affirming.

How can we remember this softer air –
the way the blackthorn twigs surrender
to the delicate dusting of bloom,
and primroses are a pale light
undimmed against fierce gorse;
the way green is pale as silver,
sharp as lime, rich as moss,
and new life unbends stiff trees.

In the long night of winter when
white stars of wood anemones,
the waxy glaze of kingcups,
do not shine, and silence
drowns the ecstatic songbirds,
we need this birth – the thin cry
to greet the mystery, insistent,
this hope born strong enough to stand.

SYERS FARM

for Della and Martin

May and the air is soft as August,
precocious summer speeding us on.
Attuned to north-eastern angles
Suffolk seems another country.
Skies stretch hot blue, fields ripple,
hedgerows breathe blossom and birdsong –
above the thatch the swallows' thin chatter –
the garden's colours overflow.

Thick walls, low ceilings hold quiet ghosts,
cool dimness perfumed with old woodsmoke,
a house where so much is growing.
Thin petals in bright light our thoughts uncurl.
We too are opening to the sun,
warming the dark parts of the heart.

SUFFOLK ANGELS

It takes some learning to live with these skies.
The first one takes your heart out from
its bony prison into your mouth where
the flutter tells you how small you are,
but alive. There is no easy contact
with horizons, space opening above,
holding the rich land down, daring your tongue
to discover the texture of firmament.
Setting timber ribs in the roofs of churches,
no wonder the craftsmen's thoughts turned to angels.
Under such skies the greatest gift is wings.
High among beams they hover, a carved host.
They will slip from bosses, ripple stiff pinions,
in Suffolk skies try out their wooden wings.

HORIZON

Better to love the violet where
sea touches sky – its hue will clear
your vision, lighten your heart again.
The blood will flow free in your veins.
It will let you cry good tears,
refill your mind with wonder.
That blue-mauve band is all the god
you need, let it dissolve the hard
sorrow, hold you like safe water
or the gentlest fingers of air.

A WOMAN WHO DREAMED

As if she had been before she saw
her cottage squat thick-walled
against the screaming wind,
the mist's damp curling;
flagged floors, dim rooms,
woodsmoke bitter-sweet.
She knew the way the mist
pearled loose-woven cloth,
clung to her hair uncoiling,
skin chafed by the heather shawl,
cold boots stiffening. She knew
other hands, knotted red,
distorted, rough with work.
The soil was thin, storms
scattered the frail new growth.
Still she planted, coaxed, tuned
to the weather's faithlessness.
Words were not her way.
She did not trust to talk.
She understood the clouds,
read the sky's meaning.
The rhythm of the sea
she carried like a pulse within.
Flowers were her joy,
colours pure and certain
in the smallest blooms.
She watched for sea pinks,
the colour soft, the flower heads
tough in salt wind and spray.
They came with summer,
when the earth relented.
They touched like love,
the sea pinks.

OUT OF EARSHOT

There is only this field, the summer
dry and hot, only this narrow path
through the crop. Underfoot the earth cracks.
Stalks like reeds are cool against bare legs.
Stretch out your arms, run your fingers
through the sea of grain. It is feathery,
rippling, not toughened yet for harvest.
You were a child here, still at the field's centre,
watching the air ruffle the surface,
waves shifting and rustling as far as
you could see, up to your armpits in green.
There at the centre you would crouch below
the surface, staring at the lines of stalks
stretching away, thin passages between,
radiating out from you, broken
sometimes, by an animal's wild swerve.
Chin on your knees in the green depths,
this is the place that comes back as comfort,
the smell of earth and your own summer skin,
the grain's swish lulling you. Alone.

VERTIGO

An old fear is stirring on the season's
turn, with this late August falter in

the rhythm. The midday sun has lost heat.
The sky gapes wide without the swifts wheeling.

She is frozen on one side of a drop.
Both feet are fixed upon one stepping stone

as her body tries to find its balance,
panic's black wings flapping in her head.

So was her child-perception true – time
a linear progression of stops and starts.

The pattern on the page, the finite words
and spaces, gave her gaps between seasons,

between Sunday and Monday, between one
year's end and the next beginning, gaps

like the ones in the open stairs that she
might not bridge, that she might fall through,

infinite and out of time. Grown up, she
should imagine joins, unbroken rhythms,

cycles and continuity, not this
gathering together for the leap across.

CRAFT

What kind of craft is this –
its timber breathes and sighs
the measure of so many seas.

The plank seat curves to hold me.
I will be pilot and I'll take the oars.
If there were a sail I would unfurl it.

No room here for another soul and
I afraid of waves, the swell
that could unsettle the safe harbour.

The rope is furred and matted.
Other hands have felt its tug, its burn,
as the grey slabs of jetty pull away.

The coils sink stiff and heavy
with departure. Will my hands coax
it to a sudden snaking curl –

deft hands, their cracks and sores healed over –
rusty rings of the jetty pulling near,
returning, and the gulls wheeling?

The boat strains for the open sea.
The only rhythm now this lift and fall,
this wooden craft is all.

REMEMBERING

Against the stark and random –
this new death, new absence –
I need the earth's quiet rhythm.

Taught the way of silence,
how to close the heart to fear,
bury pain in pretence,

I want to sing of loss, tear
the dying light with a bird's
pure notes, weep and remember.

I want a constancy – not words –
for her; rock holding safe
a million years a fern frond;

the small shelled ammonite
become eternity,
pressed in perpetual clarity.

Can I print a memory,
catch the fleeting, fading,
engrave her deep in me,

her image safe from time's eroding,
certain as the sharp stars' light.

PASSAGE

I do not want to let this woman go.
Her erratic rhythms are familiar now.
I cherish her desire's sharp knives.

I know the acrobatics of her wild joy,
a summer evening swift that plummets
to the darkest level of dumb soul.

She can be the watchful girl, washed
up warm in shallows, salty, drowned,
skin's shiver tongue-touched, mouth numb;

or the woman wondering at her body's
lore, stroking the head that bruised its way
insistent through her narrow path.

I've seen her settle into softness,
skin giving; her breasts ache in their final
ripeness. Her sex is a dark tide.

The woman in the shadows has come too soon.
Suppose her arms are whittled sticks,
her river beds quite dry?

CHANGING FRUIT

It was a pumpkin once, that belly,
stretched drum-tight, ticking with life.
She strutted amazed, oiled its surface,
remembered a girl with hip bones,
stomach muscles flat and hard.
It was a globe slow ripening.

She thinks of apples kept over for the winter,
the way tight skins begin to give,
let the bite sink in. The flesh smells sweet,
a scent to breathe in, rub against the cheek.
With this new puckering of the midriff
she will think of apples softening.

BICYCLE

What I remember is her certainty,
the steady hands that fitted, twisted, pumped,
filling the dusty tyres with rhythmic puffs;
the way she checked the brakes, then wheeled
the ticking bike into the back. She shut
the door on everything, took nothing.
She had a straight spine as she pedalled.
The lane was rutted, tussocked, trodden rough.
The adolescent bull calves danced away
from her, all tossing heads and blackberry eyes.
Hedges pushed out bramble arms, spiney fingers
clutched at her passing. She saw sunlight
tunnelled in the walled lane, glistening fruit's
soft slow ripening, sweeter than desire.

SNAPSHOT

You frown at the camera, into the sun.
Pale curls tickle your hot shoulders,
fat cherub with a sunbonnet halo.
Your costume stretches elasticated bubbles
over a two-year-old paunch. There is
the gritty damp of sand between your toes.

I know the place, not yet the child.
Narrow sand strips between shingle banks,
slippery breakwaters, the first landscape;
close up the pebbles show the tacky stain,
tar from the estuary, along the island
clay cliffs are cracking, crumbling to the sea.

I know the other girl kneeling behind you.
Serious, olive-skinned, and angular,
hair hidden by the rubber cap, she's frowning too.
You are a pale plump ball beside her,
dimpled knees, the baby crease a bracelet
at your wrist; soft shellfish with no shell.

You turn to the voice that calls, the eye
that watches as the camera clicks.
The summer afternoon shines and murmurs.
Behind, you feel the sister who does not
like you, her shadow shivers your warm skin.
You hold back watchful, and will not talk.

GHOSTS

The ghosts that haunt us are an ill-matched pair.
Our old selves at thirteen could not have known
this friendship. I would have thought you posh.
You would have thought me common. Close touch
unravels years, uncovering lost tracks.

When you were thirteen your mother sent you
away from her to school, to misery,
hundreds of miles. I see you pale and proud,
your high brainy forehead, your veiled eyes
denying the tremor of your mouth, obedient.

When I was thirteen already masking
pain in hair dye, lipstick, sulky silence,
my mother went away from me, taking
all warmth and colour. She left me nightmares,
a head full of whispers, missing, missing.

Skin to skin we conjured up these girls,
still hopelessly thirteen despite the years.
Accusing. Yours feels I pack her off,
mine that you dump her. We'll introduce them.
They can argue, blame their mothers. We'll
slip away together, find a different track.

ISLAND

for Pamela

The Ferry Road

Welcome to the sunny Isle of Sheppey,
the signboard said, a smiling yellow sun
on blue, without a hint of irony.
It's gone now. The river Swale still runs
below the bridge. The marshland shines with pools.
Sheep huddle on small mounds, chew grey-green grass.
Wind from the east tastes salt. A lapwing curls
up from the tussocks. Light catches lines of cars,
freight to be shipped, silhouetted cranes, smoke
from factories on the rim of the wild land.
There's no one left to visit, but the ghosts
crowd in. We are like pilgrims, island
children coming back to search for treasure,
in the past's east wind, dredging the estuary.

Warden Point

Farmland edges up to holiday parks.
Signs shout of chalets, golf and sea views.
Today the grey sea licks grey sky, lurks
at the cliff's base as if we did not know
it had washed away houses, the road's end.
Winter fields are furrowed purple, frosted,
stretching flats disturbed by the bend
of poplar rows breaking the wind's speed.
Natives, we know to leave the road soon, before
its plunge into the sea. We learnt the cracks,
the tarmac folding under wheels, the lure
of edges. This is unsafe ground, deep tracked
by memory. The flat land looks quiescent,
uniform. Neat fields keep close its violent drop.

Hillcrest

There are no trees now to shut out the light.
The house has shrunk. Its old bones settled.
It hunches in a dead garden, the bright
orange of its tiles bruised to a dull red.
The gaps in the rows are letting in fear.
Someone threw out the wooden name he carved.
We want to find nothing changed here,
to go back, click open the gate beside
the flowering cherry, climb the three steps,
slip into the dark hall, the wireless drone
saying he's in the kitchen, then stop
to listen for her laughter's shimmer, home.
The ghosts have gone. It is a tired house
refusing to quicken or collude with us.

FAMILIARS

Slippage

The moment holds and slows. There is something
she has forgotten. It is Sunday night.
She has not washed the blouse she needs for school.
The house is quiet and wintercold. No one there.
Fear pushes at her careful walls. The moment
slides. How did she think she was that girl?
Her sons' school shirts lie crumpled, soiled.
She must get them ready. The moment
jolts. No sons at home. No shirts. No school.
She stands unanchored. Time has dropped away.
Sunday night is a sudden abyss.
In the space between the stars she does not know
if the moments will link up again, will click
her back on track, make somewhere of nowhere.

Continental Drift

Familiarity works at below surface
level – his walk in a crowd she'd recognise
before she saw him, and then surprise
as the different images over years
coalesce to this one. But inside is
strange territory. He's crossed boundaries,
left her back on the fault-line, she squints
but doesn't see what he sees. His geology has
shifted; he's found another layer, rare
blue air her lungs don't recognise.

A habit laid down over years, she brings
with morning tea news headlines – lies, betrayals,
political gaffes to share – and hesitates,
unsure suddenly, how they look from there.

Shape-shifting

The fears change shape with years, so simple
the everyday dangers of swings and falls
now that his world is bigger than hers.
The first wish stays the same, for bright
optimism to last, anticipation
not to burn out, may time for once not dull
the clear-skyed vision of being young.
His seventeen-year-old danger mix, she's learnt,
hurt overlaid by too much beer, and she can touch
the anger in the air around him, can predict the flip
that sends bottles, chairs, against the wall,
with the force of six foot, twelve stone. In
charged air she sees again the child who knew
each day would open as a rare flower.

Distance Vision

Like a tunnel, like looking through a telescope,
at the far end of a corridor I see my sons
trying on their grown-up suits, man-sized and serious.
I see the shrug, the shoulder-shift that gets
the fit right, such certain movements, such straight backs.
Is it for another funeral that they wear these clothes,
another ritual, farewell, another parting?
I know that my way lies the other way along
the corridor. I can salute them first then turn
towards the door ahead of me. It opens outwards.
Before I touch it I have seen what happens next.
I've even seen the sunshine and the blue blue sky.
I open it. I step, and there will be no ground
at all under my feet, nothing but air to tread.

Time Travel

My mother comes to visit from the dead.
Her dead clothes are a black cloche hat, a dusty coat,
all fire and colour drained and tired, the journey was
a long one. I nurse her, give her the grandsons
she should have known. She gathers strength enough
to explore with me a city full of flights of stairs,
grey narrow mazes where we search for something.
And then I lose her. Up steep steps I run wild and sobbing
for the small dusty woman who has come so far.
'You were on the wrong stairs,' she says, smiling.
In the street the sun is shining, buildings are golden.
A clock chimes the quarter. 'My train back leaves
at ten to.' That I could let her miss it wakes me
back in the stretching desert of my loss.

Focus

Once days were single-focused. Today was
clear, as yesterday was losing definition,
tomorrow beginning to take shape. Now
every day is layered, shadowed by the skins
of other days. No day is simply that day.
Familiar faces flicker with their own ghosts.
Young men, close strangers, known by heart,
incorporate the boys they have outgrown.
The toddler absorbed in towers of swaying bricks
is in the man abstracted by the screen,
his glance reflects the mystery of distance;
this face has sharpened out of rounded cheeks,
the light that soars him on from dream to dream
is the same: eyes, like stars, are the still focus.

Trunk Call

She is a bright spot circled in time's lens.
Her head is bent, her hair conceals her face.
The words in her mother's far-off voice
are metallic sounds that do not link.
Her back hunches against their meaning.
And I from here can change nothing.
If I could tell her what will happen next
could I stop the wave from cresting higher,
pulling her out to the deepest water?
'You will not drown.' That I could say.
'You will not be a strong swimmer. Stay
in the shallows where you can see the rocks.'
Her stiff back troubles me. How thin
her shoulders look, for all that pain.

EASY RIDER

Because her innocence alarmed me
(At 63 her eyes were wide and blue)
I took my mother to see *Easy Rider*.
'You don't think people are like that really?'
The shiny carapace I'd grown at twenty
creaked, but held. I had to think it.

I'd like to phone her now to say
'Sorry about that film.' We could laugh.
Cry maybe, twenty-five years on.
I could admit how I avoid the films
that sear my eyes with hate, with hurt.
I could admit my search for candle flames
in darkness, how wrong I was, that what
I took for innocence was hope.

MY FATHER'S DREAMS

A brown berry of a man, bald head
burnished by days of gardening,
he spoke with his hands, gave each task
complete concentration, complete care.
People he avoided. I never knew
what his grey eyes saw.

Love was declared in a doll's house,
a circus ring, fitted out to
the smallest monkey. Later in golden
pie crusts, beef curled exact around
a nub of kidney. Twenty
Benson and Hedges left for me.

He didn't deal in words except
when visited by his rare dreams.
They unfurled with the complexity
of a Victorian novel, plot
enclosing plot, a narrative
that twisted down real streets,

conjured characters who spoke
through his quiet voice, mouth scarcely
moving, mysterious. I sat as
worlds crammed into minutes' sleep
unfolded in his words, a perfect plot
curled to its resolution.

'So that is what my father dreams,'
the wonder of it in my head all day,
walking back from school at night
through the unexpected places of his mind.

ARCHIVE

They found the box of letters when she died,
a lifetime mapped by pages in a clear
round hand. They spanned a half a century.
The nieces in their forties seized them up.
Family history, a woman's voice,
a record of the time, invaluable.
But it was a great niece who read them,
one heavy summer when she didn't know
who or where she was. She breathed the rhythm,
learned the language of her great aunt's mind.

At first she didn't question how the letters
were collected, she let the voice speak
to her. *I sat late into the night*
reflecting on the vastness of the sky,
the far bright stars that make my solitude
as nothing. And yet I yearn for something
to give my solitary hours new life.
Not someone. For unless you return
to haunt me I will choose no company.
Would you be a gentle ghost, my Eleanor?

She did not understand the story,
wanting answers to her questions, new paths.
As I turned the soil and planted I knew
that work is the solution for all ills.
The melancholy that takes hold of me
melts in the sunshine of productive work.
Why do I not remember that and learn
a passage through dark doubt and misery?
Yet it is hard to keep faith without you.

Why did her great aunt have the letters
she had written to her friend? A quiet love
tracked the pages week by week over
fifty years. *There is so much, as ever,*
that I want to tell you. Today the swallows
returned and with them summer, soft air
releasing winter's grip. Nature has no
hesitation in her cycles. Death is
a preparation for rebirth, new life.
But I have not found a way past death.

It was a long time before she found
the pencilled clue. *E B nineteen-ten to*
nineteen-thirty-two. The first letter's
first words slipped into place. *Dear Eleanor,*
the new year breaks bright as a promise,
but what is nineteen thirty-three to me?
Great niece Elizabeth sealed up the box,
told no one. The summer turned to autumn.
She kept her great aunt with her, a story
bitter-sweet as rosemary, as rue.

LETTER

Through the high small window
I see the moon grow towards the full.
The sky is a pale washed blue.
I cannot see the colours of the earth.

I know that I was chosen, Mother,
because of the words that my lips uttered,
so serious and strange, they said,
a gift to be given to God.

Fourth daughter, fourth try
for a son, and then he followed,
our brother who would work the land,
take the earth in his hand as his.

Husbands are hard to come by,
'And she's a strange one,' they said.
Why did you heed them, Mother?
What was it you feared?

They watched me as I sang
beside the hedges, lay in the meadow
fed by the music of birds.
I touched the wildcat, they watched.

The dart of the stiff-tailed wren,
the leaping twist of the hare,
the swallow's sudden skim stirred
the joy that gave me words.

When I ran out under the full moon,
singing my songs to the white light,
you were afraid of me, Mother.
You heeded their words.

I have dreamed of the meadow,
the hedges alive with song.
I wake tight-covered in my narrow room.
My voice is still.

My sisters lift their hearts in prayer.
My heart is stone, no words
stir in me. I have no gift
for God, Mother, in these narrow walls.

No words will reach you.
Through the high small window
I watch the sky, Mother.
I cannot see the colours of the earth.

BOY

A poem in four voices

1

He has eyes like stone, my son,
a blank grey gaze that chills.
What is it that has snuffed out
childhood? I don't know where he is.
How can I say I don't, that
I can't even talk to him? They say
'You've got to show who's boss,
Mrs Hills,' as if it's simple.
They don't know he's shut the door.
Somedays I shout as if I could
batter a way through to him,
or I try to think of things
to make him laugh. He's a kid,
after all. He's closed up tight.
One tea time I got in later
I heard him talking, like before.
He was with the little ones,
playing. When he saw me his eyes
changed. Blank. I am afraid for him.

2

At night the shadow on the wall
is Richard Cross, his big hands
coming to break my hands, snap
my wrists, if I don't get back
to him in time, and the money's
not enough, or if I tell.

Why won't my mum stop it
happening? Why won't she go
round his house, tell his dad?
Why won't she make me go to school?
But Richard Cross would tell
about the cars and the other stuff.
They'd shut me up, he says.
I'd be put away for years.
Then I couldn't creep at night
to the babies' room, lie there
curled up hearing them breathe,
smelling them all clean asleep,
wanting the day to never come.

3

His primary school report was good.
A lively boy. Responsible.
Attendance good. He started well
with us but somehow lost his way.
Persistent absences this term.
He's far behind. The mother has
been told. He lives on the estate.
The eldest child – two much younger –
different father, we presume.
The mother works. There is no
father in the household. The boy
needs discipline. He doesn't
seem to recognise that truancy
will not be tolerated. He
needs stability. The mother
shows concern but lacks authority.

4

For once before the official way,
for once before the reports, the files,
the profiles, questions, decisions,
before the blank gaze sets, may
something break the mother's sleep,
send her to open the bedroom door
to find the bed is empty. May she
stand in the doorway of the other room,
see him curled tight on the floor
between the cots where the babies sleep.
May the gentle touch of the cover
she places over him wake him
only enough for her arms, her
cheek on his cold face. May the night
release the words that will save him.
For once may this be the way it ends.

GONE FOR A SOLDIER

Absence is an open wound.
Time ricochets. I hear
the urgency of 'Mam! Mam!'
home from school to tell me,
then in the night I jerk
awake thinking I hear
him crying. The house is silent.
Loss stretches wide as a scream.

I'm afraid of sleep,
relaxing vigilance
before the dreams assault.
It's then the pictures come.
He's two, he's seven, twelve,
and then eighteen and sleeping,
face relaxed, an arm thrown back,
the skin is soft, so soft.

I thought at first he'd gone
south for work, we've people there.
He would have been afraid
to say – me always talking peace.
I haven't touched his room,
scarred walls, old picture books,
the ram's skull staring.
I keep the door wide open.

I'm afraid of letters.
My hands stutter, won't tear.
There's nothing I haven't faced
and faced. It's not just his hurt,
it's what the uniform,
the picking up a gun may do.
All those young men, hearts
hardening, no tears, forgetting.
And their mothers,
not knowing anymore who.

IT WAS AFTERWARDS

when it was quiet enough for the night
to unfurl its soft sounds, small animal
scuffle, dry click of a beetle across
the concrete, the beat of heavy wings –

after they had gone, leaving one to clean,
to wash down the walls, to rub the mop head
over and over the stain on the floor,
the shadow that the water would not shift –

long after his fear was a smell that hit
the backs of their throats, his bones their matchsticks,
his body switched on, switched off, fine wires
shrilling pain, his mind melting, red, black –

it was after he prayed who knew no god,
he screamed who knew no hope, his life fluttered
pale moth too near the flame, and the youngest
could see no more, ran out to the blank night –

long after his life – with its small mistakes,
its glimpses of understanding, memories
gathered, a scrapbook of pressed flowers –
was stamped out, discarded, disposed of –

that the clean letter came from another
world, its words unwavering, its message
anticipating only obedience,
'Let him go' it said 'He is not the one.'

MORNING

These early morning couples shine
as if they had been dipped into
a cool bright stream. They are children
lit by Christmas lights, by snow.

They walk together with their bodies new,
touched into unfamiliar sense
by fingers, tongues, held carefully.
Their eyes are afraid of morning light.

Dazed, they do not know how to carry
this knowledge with their text books, files,
how to be wise in seminars with
the skin still shivering with surprise.

They think we cannot see it, do not know.
As if our sober selves did not contain
the dizzy wonder of new passion,
the indelible tremor of the heart.

LARKIN AT F.E. COLLEGE

They tolerate this poetry, just.
School does not bring to most a love of it.
The twists and turns of language seem a test –
'Why don't they just get on and say it,
instead of making it a puzzle to unpick?'
And yet they settle, listen, watch
for metaphors and similes, the tricks
they've learnt, mechanical, detached.

I like their atmosphere, their tolerance,
the shrugs, the wandering thoughts, the little use
they really have just now for poetry.
Late nights don't dull them. They can choose
both worlds, to drink and love and dance
by night, by day to huddle over books and study.

I wonder what he would have made of them?
Would he have had the time for them that they,
willing enough, perforce are giving him,
sifting his words for what he has to say?
Youth has a brittle brightness, a fragile
purpose caught on that track between –
the child still there inside, shrinking, while
an adult hesitates, waits, remains half-seen.

What can he tell them of the adult state?
We gather words like resignation,
understated, bleak, inevitable.
They do not understand,
and I don't know the explanation.
For what I'd tell is hope, what's possible,
emotion deeply lived, and not too late.

ADULT EDUCATION

Spry the white-haired man with memories –
Mosley's fascists in Whitechapel – years
behind him giving an authority
over me to whom he is shyly deferring.

Tentative and beautiful with age,
skin sculpts an eggshell edge of bone,
a heavy-lidded grace, her eyes kindle,
light, with her mind's bold flight.

My life is a shallow pool.
I dredge the silt for shells
to offer these whose lives
stretch back behind them like the sea.

ST OSWALD'S

for David

The corners of this empty church
hold more than darkness. Bach's
harmonies lift, soar sane as sunlight.
The shadows quicken with chill breath.
It cannot be that souls are gathered here,
drawn like erratic moths by holiness.
These stone walls have absorbed
the pleas and tears of centuries.
Such music calls out from the plaster
the dumb shapes of dark sorrow.
It promises sweet order, to calm
the unquiet heart, the random pain.
The air is thick with old grief,
the restless flutter of unsettled prayer.

LONDON

The throng around this case attracts where
room after room is filled with artefacts.

In dim light the bog man curls on his side,
his leathery knees drawn to his chin.

He is thin. His flesh did not endure.
His face is sharpened to bone, to pain.

He did not have a comfortable death.
There is no peace for him in this place either.

Outside the Underground a boy sits
motionless. His eyes are dry stones.

Dusk fills the hollows of his cheeks.
His skin is grey, his chin rests on his knees.

He is still upright. That his flesh has not
lasted does not draw wondering crowds.

His case is usual in this city where
bright posters warn us not to give.

THE TOUR

This is the city. Yes, people once lived here.
The heaps of rubble were homes, workplaces.
No, there were proper buildings – tall houses,
offices, hospitals, museums, shops.
Yes. They were people living ordinary lives.

Those are the remains of the bodies
that fell in the streets. No. The custom here
too was to bury the dead, to give them
respect, mark their passing with ritual.
The ordinary patterns have been lost.

Yes, the stench is sickening to my nose.
I do not know if I am shocked. Once I was
shocked. Up here are the camps where the living
wait. Those for whom you search may be here.
I do not know how many are waiting.

No, of course we have children too. Look there,
that is a child, and those huddled there,
they are children. Yes, here too, parents cared
for children. Now these care for themselves.
No, I assure you they are not old people.

Yes, all are hungry. Once this race was sturdy,
straight backs, strong limbs. Yes, I can see that
you do not believe me. The leaders? Who knows.
They are dead. They have escaped. They are hiding.
The only certainty is that they are not here.

Yes, as far as you can see the camp stretches,
then further. Perhaps you will not find them here.
Yes, it might be better to look no further.
When you get home, yes, you could write to the papers.
No, of course there is no more you can do.

WAR FILMS

Those archive films of trenches have
a kind of innocence about them now:

uniforms, battlefields, officers; battles
that began and ended, combat rules.

Our footage is the family mortared at their meal.
War blasts apart each private ritual.

The simple acts of daily life are targetted –
an old man shopping, a child running –

picked off by the sniper who watches
from the edges of the ordinary.

Our century has been advanced in horror.
We married up technology

with systematic hate, distanced death,
computerised the carnage.

The anonymity we made of war
could not prepare us for this:

that in our private lives we feel
the wind's cold blast,

humanity's straw walls blazing
in an endless dark.

SEVEN NINETY-THREE

Sleep never comes   sealing these lids
open-eyed I watch   weep out time
witness the world   in wintercold future

So many winters and the colours stay.
The coast is deeper-mouthed, the bays
bite back further in the soft dunes.
The grass is a dry whisper in the wind,
now as then; the grey-beige sand
ripples with its own waves, and
the sea knows nothing, or everything.

Mine was a time of spells, of faith.
We knew strange powers, feared curses,
believed in healing. Our vision
was inward. Our fears were small,
our hopes within reach. What
we knew of strife was in old tales.
Ours was a quiet time, before the fires.

I have wandered this coastline
from then until now. I cannot rest.
I cannot cease. You must believe me.
Listen. I will give you my spell,
my prayer, my warning. Beware
invaders from the sea, from the sky.
They will cross borders with fire.

They will burn the place of learning,
destroy what the imagination
in peace created. Beware
all justification of hate,
all glorification of brute strength.
Beware the desire for power.
Beware complacency and disbelief.

What I have seen would break
the human frame, split the heart.
I could tell you that we do not learn.
We have made the world change, yet
we repeat, repeat, as the sea rears
in grey salt walls, smashes to spray
to lips of foam, now as then.

*

The roar of this grey sea has always
meant home, the wind in the marram,
the dipping dunes. Before the fear came
our life was hard and simple, tied to
earth and sea. Beasts were raised, grain cut,
the waters fished. My father worked the land.
My mother spun grey fleeces to fine thread.

She taught me her craft. From childhood
I understood that everything we had
was necessary. There was nothing spare.
A day's work was dictated by
the season, weather, tide, each one of us
had tasks that meshed with others' tasks.
The rhythm of our lives was clear.

The sea was our pulse. It fed us, gave us work.
Its creatures and its precious salt
made our small settlement rich enough.
We carried inland fresh fish to exchange
for goods, the foods we could not grow.
We heard about far lands across the sea,
brave voyagers to holy places.

Whether the grain would ripen, whether
the sheep would lamb, whether enough
had been set by to see us through
the cold dark months, these were
our deepest matters. We had our tragedies.
Our children died. Love turned to hate.
Perhaps all dreams have common shape.

*

Our people by the shore, the holy men
gathered on the island, were all I knew
except the travelling traders, the singers,
who passed through. The monastery drew me.
It was a peaceful place, a world of men,
who worked like us, yet knew strange crafts.
The meaning of their life was closed to me.

Sometimes a boy from our settlement
was taken there, taught the ways of god.
We visited with skins for trade, steering
our cart along the causeway at low tide.
They sowed their crops, and harvested,
reared beasts and slaughtered them,
but their lives ran to another pattern.

The worship of their god was first.
They left their other tasks to pray,
to gather to their offices, sing and chant.
I listened to their music outside
the wall, stirred strangely by the sound,
order and sweet harmony beside
the storm, the seabirds' sorrowful call.

It was not their god I sought; their buildings
were a miracle. I watched once where a man
sat in a pool of light, setting colours
like the purest flower tints into patterns.
I think he sat the whole day at that work.
I loved the light room, the space they held
within their walls, the high roof beams.

I envied him his quiet task,
the delicate shapes, fine lines he made,
the care his fingers took. My fingers'
tips were hard with cold, grease from
the fleeces thickened them. My threads
were grey as winter sky, no blue
like gentian, red like poppy, no fine gold.

*

the old works of the giants stood desolate

We knew there was a bigger world,
that men had lived another way,
bringing in times past stone-building
skills from across the seas. No wonder
to you, to us who built in wood
stone cities seemed the work of giants,
their empty streets a portent.

The singers told us of the ruins,
of buildings bigger than the priory's,
slabs cut and shaped, ranged high.
How would it be to sleep within
a weight of stone? I never slept beneath
the timbers of our meeting hall.
I choose to lie where I can see the night.

I listened till I almost saw
those cities, the wonders that they held –
the pictures made of coloured stones
bright as pebbles, tossed and glistening
at the waves' lip; the way the walls bore
heated water, warming air without a fire;
surfaces like milk covering the earth.

I dreamed I trod those floors, I touched
what they had made. They were not like us.
We could not know the meaning of their lives,
the certainty they cut and dressed in stone,
the thoughts laid out in solid shapes.
The cities stood, deserted monuments
full of ghosts to frighten us. Warning.

The empty halls, the silent buildings
told us that such giants fail,
however grand their dreams, however
beautiful their execution. We did
not heed. Curiosity succeeded fear.
In time the desolation ceased to move,
but drew our people to their walls.

Nibbling at the edges, scuttling
among ruins, scavenging what
could be used, without understanding,
our people took what they could carry,
fragments of another world.
In our squat churches sit great stones
that have known a loftier place.

And did we set the seeds of desolation
with new ambition, catching the shadow
of a dream, an echo of the pride that
rates a building higher than the cliff
where foam mists and the calling seabirds nest?
What purpose drives the temple builder,
what purpose the holy man in his pool of light?

*

Looking for causes beyond the greed,
the drive for territory, for power,
I think we lived a mole-blind life,
tunnelling a way close to the earth,
coming up for air and never thinking.
Now I cannot remember her, Eardstapa,
spinner of fine wool, in her time of peace.

I can see now what was hidden then,
the signs that other purposes
had failed, that invaders had come once,
could come again across the seas.
The minstrels sang of battles, sieges,
warlike ambition, and we listened,
as if such happenings were dreams.

Poor little settlement, our enemies
only the bad harvest, blight,
strange sicknesses that took the old,
the children. We marked our festivals,
expected little. How often it is said,
we did not expect such a thing to happen.
Blind moles tunnelling at life.

*

We called him Plover, a broken boy,
leg slow dragging like an injured wing,
he limped the shoreline, watching nets,
sea-harvesting most curious shells.
He knew the tides and currents, when
the storm would break, the wind cease.
Yet that day we did not believe him.

(You will have known such a boy,
driven into dreams, a thinker,
left behind in the children's games.
But his words were bright pictures
that all could look on when light
faded and we gathered round the fire.
Why did we not believe him?)

He said he saw a creature sliding
on the surface of the sea, shining
bird head, wings or legs in rhythm
swimming fast, lined bumps like backbone,
regular and shining. He said he saw
another following, then others, strange
shoal of fish-bird creatures.

We laughed, suspected him of tales
to catch the ears of adults. No fisherman
had seen such sea-life, a fish
with insect legs, a bird unfeathered,
bright and smooth. He shook, the broken boy,
he said he had no cause to lie, he swore
by his strange shoal. We did not listen.

They must have come again. Perhaps he knew
but did not trust to us the telling.
If only one of us had trusted him
we might have asked the holy men.
We asked them about many things
we did not understand, the quiet men
on the island working with their god.

The day of the first fires, we called it.
Nothing marked it out, the sun rose.
No god put out the light to save them.
I do not know who heard him first,
wild calls outcried the waves' roar
high up the shore – 'The island is on fire.'
I saw the dark smoke gathered in a pall.

Men ran for boats. High tide concealed
the crossing. On the shore the women waited.
It was then we saw the glint, the rhythm,
fat-swimming shoal beyond the island.
We knew it for a fleet, an enemy
from another land across other seas.
We saw our safety pass with them.

The stories that the men brought back
would not surprise you. You know it all.
I cannot find words for a broken world –
those men were peaceful, unarmed, serious.
What had they done to be so butchered?
Something left our world then, something new
came in. First knowledge seems the worst, at first.

*

Afterwards we learned of other warnings
missed. Our eyes were occupied with
daily tasks, small work. Had we looked up
we might have seen the fiery dragons.
The lack of food we took as our bad
husbandry. We were earth-bound people
with little time for higher purposes.

Such happenings belonged in songs, old tales.
We could not dream that giants would come
across the sea to harm us in our little lives.
We had no riches. We were not kings.
They came with axes and with fire.
The sea that fed us gave them passage.
Our rhythm faltered then, was lost.

You know the hankering for innocence,
the looking backwards to a time when –
We wanted ignorance, to forget
the screams of children in a burning hut,
the mad cries of the woman who cannot
cleanse her thighs of blood, the head
that grins and stares from the ditch.

Murder we knew and the strength of fire.
There had been feuds and quarrels.
We used to quiet the children's
nightmares after tales of battle, now
we lived the nightmare, fear
stealing sleep from us, breaking
apart the daily patterns.

Some said we had displeased the gods –
the old gods – the new god – great
wickedness was in our midst, to be
cauterised by this enemy.
We eyed each other secretly.
Who had brought this to us, for whose
hidden evil did we burn?

We learned vigilance, to watch
the sea, the dunes, at every hour.
We sharpened blades, resolved to kill.
What they would take we must defend.
They took our life from us, transformed
our dreams. They taught despair and hatred,
turned our eyes outwards to horizons.

*

You will find no traces of us now.
A settlement like ours could not survive.
We were not practised in the skills
required against that enemy.
We were so few, and most of us
no fighters. We had our old, our weak,
our children. They came as warriors.

I, Eardstapa, spinner of fine thread
died in my forty-seventh year.
What happened here has happened
always. That day I travelled south
for trade, taking my woollen thread
to a weaver in another place.
The sun was sinking as I returned.

From the cliff top I saw the fire.
The wind blew the cries away from me,
but I knew them. I had seen
the split skulls, the women broken.
I saw the longboats beached beyond
the look-out, and then the Northmen
climbing the path towards me.

I chose my own way. Nothing
would be left of our frugal life;
the huts we built, the meeting hall,
the nets at the shoreline, the salt-pans,
our careful husbandry, our people.
I let the men get close to me.
I spread my arms and leapt.

No kittiwake to skim and hover,
hugging the cliff face for a safe ledge,
my body dropped, broke upon the rocks
below. Salt purifies. The tide
sucked, tumbled the heavy flesh
into the wave's curl, the green deep.
But my spirit could not leave this shore.

ove across black rocks at dawn,
the cold air that once blued my legs does
no harm now. The pain I thought lay
in my heart lives on with me, as if
to punish. The spirit is troubled
always. With the crying seabirds
the cliff face is a kind of haven.

A winter sky has much to teach us.
February grey waves beating, breaking.
Any answer would lie there, not
with humanity. I have witnessed
too much time. It is a gritty wind
and the soul's eyes cannot close,
or blink with eyelids burned away.